to make
monsters
out of girls

to make
monsters
out of girls

amanda lovelace

Andrews McMeel
PUBLISHING®

books by amanda lovelace

the
WOMEN ARE SOME KIND of MAGIC™
series:

the princess saves herself in this one (#1)
the witch doesn't burn in this one (#2)

***

the
things that h(a)unt
duology:

to make monsters out of girls (#1)

note from the author

this book originally appeared on wattpad in chapbook form under the title *poetry will not make you immortal*. the book you're holding now, *to make monsters out of girls*, is the same story you read then, only it has been edited, expanded upon, illustrated, & given a new & more fitting title. thank you, lovely readers, for reaching out & for inspiring me to bring my creation to its full potential.

laced with love,
amanda

this is dedicated
to the one who
stepped back
& let me
grow.

trigger warning

intimate partner abuse,
eating disorders,
self-harm,
cheating,
alcohol,
religion,
death,
gore,
fire,
blood,
& possibly
more.

remember to practice
self-care before,
during, & after
reading.

contents

this is the
sun-filled sky.

these are the
singing blackbirds.

these are the
empty pews.

this is the
cracked piano.

this is the
choking choir.

these are the
withered roses.

this is my
little black dress.

these are my
tear-dry cheeks.

this is my
red lipstick grin.

this is your
silent eulogy.

this is your
word-wrapped coffin.

&
this—

this is how
i will finally bury you.

- *it's much too late to repent, sweetheart.*

oh yes, i know what you're thinking, but the poems you find in this book won't immortalize you. these poems are the means by which you will finally become dead to me—licked clean from my insides like the last dollop of honey at the very bottom of the pot. everyone will finally learn what you did to me all those years ago, but none of them will ever be able to scrape the bitter taste your name leaves on my tongue . . . now will they, ███████?

- this is your unmarked grave.

monster boy

i'm
convinced
i become
transfixed
a
thousand times
in any given
day—

by smiles,
by words,
by songs,
by smells,
by flowers,
by crystals,
by raindrops,
by coffee mugs,

& even by
the things that bite.

- *my fatal flaw.*

little lovesick
me

watched
tuck everlasting on

a merry-go-round
loop

& i could never
get past the 'why'—

why why why
why why why

did winnie
refuse to drink

from the
eternal spring

that
would allow her

to go on
endless adventures

alongside her
beloved jesse?

it would
have been

just them
against this

awful
mortal world

until
the day

the earth
caught fire,

                                        & what
                                        else

                                        is there
                                        to live for

                                        besides
                                        your

                                        one true
                                        love?

- & now i would tell her, "everything."

before i met you, my darling monster-boy, i was with that shy green-eyed boy. in case you forgot, he was the one who traveled so fleetingly between me & the girl wearing the lemon sundress that i forgot he was even there most days. oh, i'm sure you remember. he was the one who stopped by every night & opened my closet—careful so as not to make a sound— so he could tuck away his knapsack filled with secrets, utterly convinced that shielding me was the same as protecting me.

- *you never thought i needed protection from your lies.*

that
green-eyed boy

may have
left me for dead

when he
walked away

with one hand
in hers,

but
it wasn't long

before
you stopped

&
offered me

a hand
d r i p p
            i
with   n
resurrection.   g

- *did i ever even have a choice?*

he
told me
i was an
obligation

like
grocery shopping
on an
empty stomach,

but you
told me
i was as
vital

as
that
after-dinner
cigarette

you
could never
have just
one of.

- *the difference between.*

i'm not sure
if this makes
any sense,
but you
make me
forget
what
it feels like
to miss
someone
i was never
allowed
to
call
mine.

- are you my antidote or my poison?

the boy
who isn't sure
about anything
is sure
about
me.

- *weak at the knees.*

(when a sad, sad girl with a mangled-up heart comes face to face with a beautiful boy who loves nothing more than mangling hearts, is there really any way it can end other than in bloodshed?)

- this story may be cliché, but it's ours.

you're
the one

who
sings

in
tongues

of
no-star nightmares.

- *we never did inhabit the same sky.*

i'm
the one

who
soothes

in
waves

of
lapis-cloud lullabies.

- *we never did inhabit the same sky II.*

we're so wrapped up in each other that we begin to miss meals. we can't sleep for more than a few hours at a time. we forget everything that makes us ache in the worst ways. we're so afraid this will all slip from our fingers like a haze of barely-there smoke, so we make a kind of game out of it.

"want to play?" you ask me.

before i can answer, you explain the rules like this: "you'll bleed yourself dry for me one question at a time—no passing. i'll lick your wounds & then you'll do the same for me. right here, right now."

"who goes first?" i ask. no hesitation.

- the truth without the dare.

if you start to keep score,
can you still call it
love?

- *signs.*

falling in love
with you

was
like that

knowing,
heart-stopping,
airless,
upside-down

moment
right before

a fatal
collision.

- brace for impact.

might
as well
say "bye-bye"
because
this girl
right here
is a
fucking
goner.

- with you there is no faking it.

"i've got to tell you—that sleep-coated voice might just send me to my grave."

- this boy, he'll be the death of me.

you had years
on me
&
i wanted
to drag
my teeth
across
the surface
of every one
of them.

- red & wolf.

you had years
on me
&
i was
too young
to realize
you were the
one who
should have
known better.

- red & wolf II.

my boy—

        he doesn't sparkle.

my boy—

        he doesn't dazzle.

my boy—

        he doesn't shine.

when

        he kisses me

i can taste

        all the midnights

he doesn't

        even try to hide.

- *my monster-boy.*

he's
something
out of a
bedtime
story,

but

i have yet
to decide
if he's the
chivalrous man
come to
rescue me

or

the
ravenous
monster
come to
devour me
& leave me
screaming
in the dark.

- i don't think i'd mind either one.

we lay there in comfortable silence for several lifetimes & reincarnations before you finally break it. "how very special it is," you remark, twirling a lock of my hair around your finger, "that you had every reason to lock, bolt, & paint your door shut, but you still had enough space in that trusting heart of yours to leave it ajar & brave the cold air for me."

& i thought, *trusting? or naïve?*

- the invitation.

i rest
my head
on top of
your chest
& the song
inside
sounds
like
the
soundtrack
to my
salvation.

- i never did have an ear for music.

over & over he would tell me that i was the honey to his tea—the only thing that could ever sweeten him to his liking. somewhere along the way, he forgot to mention the swarms of flies & wasps that would eventually come to cover everything we made together. the spoilage of all this misguided longing.

- infestation.

when day breaks,
her monster
tells her
he loves
her,

not me.

when night falls,
my monster
tells me
he loves
me,

not her.

i have trouble
believing
the monster
loves
either of

us.

- god, do i ever learn?

i still can't
decide
if we
managed
to meet
at all
the
wrong times,
or
if we just
weren't
meant
to meet
at all.

- for someone who doesn't believe in fate,
i sure do write about it a lot.

the
only way
i can
remember
what
happened
is if
i sit down
&
pray
to
the paper
&
hope
the pen
is a believer.

- to make up for the fact that i'm not.

even lucifer himself wore a pair of wings on his shoulder blades, but remember, dear one—it wasn't long before he let the straps slip down & everyone found out he was never who he was always pretending to be.

- fool me once, twice, thrice.

monster girl

"do you think she knows about us?" i ask.

"'*us.*' i fucking love the sound of that."

- *you always did crave the taste of your own lies.*

this love leaves bloodstains
on my once-white
linens.

- indisputable evidence.

i'm so fucking sorry.
i'm so fucking sorry.
i'm so fucking sorry.
i'm so fucking sorry.
i'm so fucking sorry.
i'm so fucking sorry.
i'm so fucking sorry.
i'm so fucking sorry.
i'm so fucking sorry.
i'm so fucking sorry.
i'm so fucking sorry.
i'm so fucking sorry.
i'm so fucking sorry.
i'm so fucking sorry.
i'm so fucking sorry.
i'm so fucking sorry.
i'm so fucking sorry.
i'm so fucking sorry.
i'm so fucking sorry.
i'm so fucking sorry.
i'm so fucking sorry.
i'm so fucking sorry.
i'm so fucking sorry.
i'm so fucking sorry.
i'm so fucking sorry.
i'm so fucking sorry.
i'm so fucking sorry.

i'm so fucking sorry.
i'm so fucking sorry.
i'm so fucking sorry.
i'm so fucking sorry.
i'm so fucking sorry.
i'm so fucking sorry.
i'm so fucking sorry.
i'm so fucking sorry.
i'm so fucking sorry.
i'm so fucking sorry.
i'm so fucking sorry.
i'm so fucking sorry.
i'm so fucking sorry.
i'm so fucking sorry.
i'm so fucking sorry.
i'm so fucking sorry.
i'm so fucking sorry.
i'm so fucking sorry.
i'm so fucking sorry.
i'm so fucking sorry.
i'm so fucking sorry.
i'm so fucking sorry.
i'm so fucking sorry.
i'm so fucking sorry.
i'm so fucking sorry.
i'm so fucking sorry.
i'm so fucking sorry.
i'm so fucking sorry.

- what she still deserves to hear.

maybe
i didn't know

what
real love was

before you
walked in,

but what i did
know is that

it's not
supposed to

feel like
i'm waking up

choking on
p i e c e s

of my bashed-in
teeth.

- *right?*

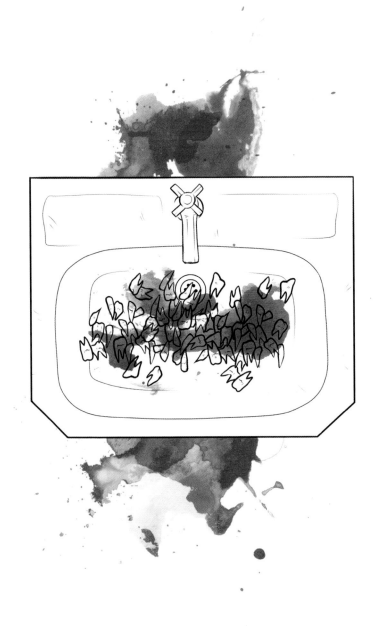

maybe
i'm such a
night owl

because of all
those mornings
you woke up
& magically
decided
you

- *no longer wanted me.*

on the days
you decided you

were still in this
with me,

ancient trees
leaned in to my touch;

will-o'-the-wisps
swarmed around me;

butterflies
made nests in my hair;

falling stars
tangled in my eyelashes;

nectar oozed
from my fingertips;

& even oceans
feared the multitudes in me.

- *moon made up of honey.*

pull out
every poem

i've
ever written

about
you

&
they'll all

have the
same

underlying
message

written
a thousand

different
ways:

i was
never ever

supposed to
crave you

~~the way~~
~~i did,~~

but
i did.

- *hunger.*

soon

"i didn't mean it."

turned into

"i never mean it."

- *it starts in the tender moments.*

the
apologies
came
so frequently
it was
exhausting
for
both of us
&
eventually
you
didn't bother
offering one
at all.

- *numb.*

on the off-chance someone ever asked me to describe you without actually describing you, i would say you are the bruises & teeth marks i find all over my body without remembering how they got there in the first place.

- this isn't a haunting; it's a hunting.

they say
if you place

a frog
in a gradually

boiling pot
of water,

they'll become
so accustomed

to the familiar
sting

that they'll
lay down

their whole
life for it.

i was
that frog,

except
i didn't need

to be
convinced

to get
into that pot.

i was
so desperate

for
a warm place

to stay
& curl up in

that i took
the leap

inside
with no

convincing
from you.

- *the cycle.*

he says to me, "darling, if loving you is such a sin
then it's probably a good thing that god forgives
sinners like me."

- *no absolution for me.*

i can't tell
the difference
between
you
&
the dead
of
winter.

- at least winter makes way for spring.

"why don't you leave him?"
they ask me.

- *the question.*

i can't decide who it is i'm more frightened of—
you, or the person i've let myself become since
knowing you. that little girl used to wake up
at dawn because she saw each day as an
adventure awaiting her? the little girl who used
to chase invisible faeries around the garden
with her grass-stained feet? the little girl who
saw magic in mundane things like mismatched
teaspoons & broken clocks?

she's so far gone, i don't think she'll ever be able
to claw her way back to me.

- *monster-girl.*

the monster
made himself
another monster
because he
couldn't stand
being a monster
all by
himself.

- & yet that weight grows heavier still.

quick!—

>   hunt down
>   all the mirrors.

quick!—

>   spider-web them
>   with your fists.

quick!—

>   erase all
>   traces of her.

if all else fails,

>   i'll chew up the
>   remaining shards.

(i've swallowed *much*

>   sharper words
>   than this.)

i can no longer

>   stomach the beast
>   staring back at me

if you're looking for your perfect victim, then you might as well set down your lanterns. you won't be able to find her here. i'm the fairy tale everyone forgot about because the lesson wasn't pure or hopeful enough. in this one, there are plenty of times when red becomes a little bit wolf after the beast comes for her with his snapping jaw too hard, too often.

- i don't excuse her & you shouldn't either.

every word
that
suicide-jumps
from
your lips
sounds
unmistakably
like
a synonym
for
"farewell."

- couldn't you at least try to hide it?

during
the breakup,
i
attended
a total
of five funerals.
the whole time,
no one knew
about all the
funerals
i was
having for you
with
each step of

my
blood-
red
stilettos.

- *i never knew you could grieve a*
  breathing man.

you remind me of the way flowers bloom so furiously in the spring, like the loudest fucking declaration of survival you'll ever witness. as if to say, "i'm back. i'm here. i'm alive. i won't waste a single second dwelling on what it's like to be anywhere else." although, you also remind me of the way flowers always—without fail—wither where they stand & slowly but surely return to the earth, particle by particle, back to the home they keep most of the year.

- *where they know they truly belonged all along.*

tell me—
are you
breaking her
like
you broke me,
or am i just that
special?

- *playing favorites.*

can you
explain to me
why
my arms
have turned
so cold
when
they never
even got
the chance
to hold
you?

because
i can't.

- *nothing makes sense with or without you.*

what you need to know about the monster:
when they threaten to disappear without a
trace, they never really do. pay close attention
next time & notice how they always leave the
door cracked open a little behind them in
fear that you won't invite them in the next time
they're feeling insecure & lonely & starved for
something more loyal than they've ever been.

- *my open door.*

he says he's done with me.
he actually means it this time.

- two sentence horror story.

truth without the dare?

every cell in my body cries that i won't be able to bring myself to show anyone else all the set-in stains on my soul, like a tour through the museum of how fucked up i am. my god, i just realized you'll be one of the tour stops now. how the hell am i supposed to cope with that? it's true what you've always told me—no one could ever want this natural disaster of a girl on their hands.

- *no one except for you.*

i'm the kind of love-exhausted a thousand years of sleeping in a glass box buried six feet under couldn't cure.

- *the snow white tale you didn't hear.*

i wish
i could say

i have finally
erased

all the pained
"i love you"s

& all the desperate
"i need you"s

whispered over
static-heavy phone lines.

try as i may,
i can't do that.

i only wish i could
let go of your

venom-dipped words
& neck-broken promises,

but these are
the kinds of memories

that were made
for the ones like me

my body didn't want to know what it was like to survive without you. for a year after, i watched that disappearing act of a girl from the corner of my bedroom ceiling, where she couldn't hear me screaming that she needed to stop depriving herself of the things she needed the most. to stop with the numbers, with the counting. even then i knew how fucked up it was, but i started to feel happy when all the parts of me that were still in love with you were dripping like nectar from my bones.

- *i am still rebuilding.*

there was
no comfort

to be
found in

the
pages

that once
pulled me

through
it all.

- *you took things i didn't know you*
  could take.

how
can you
expect me
to be friends
with you

when
the inside
of my mouth
is crusted over
with scabs

from
the effort
it takes not
to say those
three words

you never
want
to hear
from me
again?

- *"i love you" / "i hate you".*

i'm the mistake he apologizes for
only to keep

making it.
making it.
making it.
making it.
making it.
making it.

- *it seems you never learn, either.*

i may not hold much faith in god (you know i never really have, which always bothered you), but the very thought of you lurking in the nearby shadows has me filling up all my perfume bottles with holy water.

- *father, exorcise me.*

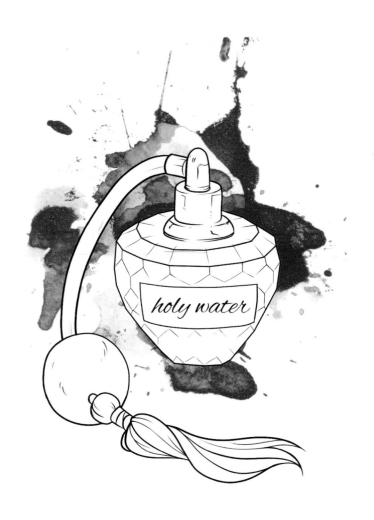

either

take
everything i have

or drop it all
& walk away.

both
are no longer

an option
i'm allowing.

you see,
it's not exactly

in this girl's
nature

to be
torn

in

two.

- indecision.

sun-heart

in the autumn, the monster ripped his way through my bosom, twisted my heart until it became a deadened thing, & buried it somewhere in the leaf-littered wood. he left no marker, no signs leading back to it. when i asked him why he did this, he told me that he was finished with it for now & he didn't want anyone else to find it in the meantime.

- the ending.

in the spring, the thawing began. with a hand clutched to my chest, i stumbled down that overgrown path, dug through the softened dirt, & took that beatless thing back into my hands. i leaned in & whispered to it, "please don't give up. not yet. there's still someone you should be beating for—me." somewhere in that darkness, the faintest sparkle of light bloomed.

- the beginning.

i crawl
i stand
i stumble
out

of
your
shadow-bursting
lair

&
with
the little
i have left,

i
stretch
my arms
wide o p e n &

i   spin
     spin
              spin
        spin

meanwhile,
the gracious sun
mumbles
between

each kiss
to my
scarred
back,

"darling, you are worthy."
"darling, you are worthy."
"darling, you are worthy."
"darling, you are worthy."

to
my surprise,
none of it
burns.

- darling, i am worthy.

once my eyes adjusted to the brightness—that's when i first noticed him. a shovel in one hand, a mud-splattered heart in the other. i waved, offering a small, hopeful grin in his direction. a cautious smile grew in return. i so desperately wanted to say to him, *you can do this, you know. you can come back from whatever it is that they did to you,* but i knew he already knew that. he didn't need any reassurances from me, just as i didn't need any from him. but if nothing else, there is so much comfort to be found in knowing that we aren't the only ones who feel like the freezing season will never relent.

- *the sun-heart.*

"but my heart—i don't know if it can love again just yet," i warn him.

"let your heart take its time," he replies, his voice surer than any i've heard before. "as it so happens, mine needs a rest, too. we're both here, anyway—we can take them both & lock them away in a box so they can figure things out together."

- closed for repairs.

i never wanted to
fall for him, & so,
in my usual
fashion,
i
d
i
d

- *hopeless & romantic.*

his name
rests
inside
my throat
like
i was
born
trying to
say
it.

- *the kind of inevitable i don't dread.*

my new love—
he's got a green thumb.

where you
neglected me

& let the weeds
overtake,

he's always
so very nurturing.

& you'll never
guess what—

he made for
damn sure

he repotted me
where i could

stretch towards
the light

& finally
outgrow you.

- *my new love is here to ruin your day.*

when i was finally feeling brave enough, i told you, "i can't do this with you anymore. if you're never going to leave me, then this is me leaving you. there's someone else seeping in through the fractures you left, & i swear he's the most honest thing i've ever known. he's not shadow-touched like i am, ~~like we are~~. it's like the sun herself radiates from his freckles."

"you don't deserve him," you replied. "& don't try to convince yourself that you ever will."

- one of the few things we agreed on.

"that girl is mine," the monster-boy growled.

"that's where you're wrong. that girl belongs to the coffee shops & the bookstores & the treetops—but mostly she just belongs to herself," he said, unafraid.

- *thank you.*

the king of games,
he called himself.

- *unlike you, he never tried to be the king of me.*

they will
make you think
every person
you meet
is wearing
a mask
to hide
their fangs.

- & they will be wrong.

&
yet . . .

how am i
supposed to believe

he's not just
wasting time with me

while he waits
for a girl who doesn't

have to
reach through the dark

to keep making sure
the other side

of the sheet
isn't turning cold?

- *trust issues.*

"you'll leave," i cried.

"only if i'm with you," he cried back.

- *guess i was good enough after all.*

he
told me
he never
learned
how to
swim;
i
told him
it
was okay
because
i did.

- i will carry him across treacherous seas.

catch me in bed
playing with matches

surrounded by
the letters

i never sent
my monster-boy.

catch me
        lighting
                    blowing out
        lighting
                    b l o w i n g   o u t
the flames

next to the sleeping
sun-heart

who sits up to
eat the fire with me

& lets the letters
remain unharmed

without having to be
asked.

- *our quiet understanding.*

i've come to
realize that

i am
always learning.

right now,
i am learning

how not to see
the image

of your face
coming through his

&
that's okay.

i know you're
somewhere

doing the same,
albeit for

very different
reasons.

- *my fear / your regret.*

moons
after it ended,
you still
snuck up
to my mailbox
to deliver
bundles
of letters—

half
love notes,
half
hate notes.

when
you found
someone new,
all your letters
came back
to you
marked
[return to sender].

- *find a new partner in crime.*

someone
i used to know

told me that
love was forever

& if you ever
feel it waning,

then it was never
truly there.

but you're
the solid,

tangible proof
that they were

dead fucking
wrong.

- *this girl has learned to love
  with conditions.*

didn't
anyone ever
warn you
not to
try
to trick
a girl
who reads?

she's
already
seen
everything.

- *don't try to waste your time again.*

i would be lying if i ever said you served no greater purpose in the book of my life. there is at least one good deed that i can attribute to you. it was only after you left me stranded & i found myself still breathing that i knew i could withstand everything that came after you— even the tempest that rattled the hinges on all the doors & blew all the shutters off & split every tree around me in half. she was nothing in comparison to you.

- *stronger than all the storms.*

i already know i shouldn't be writing these poems about you anymore. if it's any consolation, they're more about me than they are about you *(in other words: it's not you, it's me).* the only reason i'm letting myself write them now is so i can finally write about all the worthwhile things that disappeared when you sent them off to sail the foggy, forbidden sea. despite the best of your efforts, the ship found its way back to me & i've realized there is so much more to my existence than the memory of a man who would love to see me drown in search of happiness without him.

- the letter i never sent.

you're married now, but not to the first girl. not to me. no, you ended up marrying a completely different girl. that seems like it should be the punch line to a really, really bad joke after everything you put us through. after everything i contributed to.

yes, i can admit my fault now. i might have been young, but i was nowhere near blameless in the end of our dream. you're not at fault for anything i said or did—only i am.

the first time i heard the news, i expected tears. i expected a cry so loud that it would land upon stars in other galaxies. in other universes. in other dimensions. at the very least, i expected a vodka-neat scorch to rip through my body. but you know what? that didn't happen. the world did not stop mid-spin, nor did it lose a pigment of its color. the sun never became eclipsed by the all too self-important moon.

i imagine going back in time to tell my younger self about this moment—the one where i finally realize that my life truly did go on without you wreaking havoc inside of its walls. i try so hard to imagine it, but i know she wouldn't believe a single useless word i said.

yet here i am. i stand before you the woman who managed to become everything you said she could never one day be. in the years since you've been gone, i've managed to find love again; more importantly, i've managed to find myself again. now i'm the one who takes all our mistakes & sells them to strangers.

- the letter i never sent II.

just like in the movies, we quite literally bump into each other at the bookstore one afternoon. i'm not sure what kind of books you like to read anymore—probably something like stephen king—but all the ones tucked in your arms go tumbling to the ground & mix with my gillian flynn. i don't even sense them falling. i'm too mystified by the sight of you to bend down & help you pick them back up.

"why don't we grab some coffee & catch up?" you ask. so we do. you tell me stories about your children & i try to smile politely at the correct times. you avoid mentioning your wife & i avoid mentioning my spouse, which is probably best for both of us. i try to tell you about my writing & you can't hide the red draining from your cheeks, so you find a way to change the subject. no, you don't want to hear about all the hollywood monsters i turned you into to make people understand.

there is no slow blast of fireworks. there are no heartstrings finally coming to relax underneath the table between us. there is no magical moment of lost love found. inside this moment, we are not allie & noah. no, in this moment i am allie & you are lon. or maybe you are noah & i'm martha. i can't be certain.

what there is, however, is a sort of silent understanding. in a different life, we could have been holding hands across this table, discussing ordinary things like grocery lists & who will pick which child up from what at which time, but in the life we currently occupy, we're two almost-strangers struggling as we try not to look at each other too closely while we pick the splintered apologies out from the cramped space between our teeth.

in this life, you want to tell me, "i'm sorry i didn't know how to stop the pretending."

in this life, i want to tell you, "it's all right. i'm sorry i let you stay despite the pretending."

(none of this ever happened.)

- the letter i never sent III.

i can
no longer
remember how
warm your
nicotine laugh
felt
when it
slid through
me.

- *how to know when it's really over.*

i am
no longer
allowed
to know
who you
are,
yet
i sleep
soundly.

- how to know when it's really over II.

in
the act
of
putting you
before
myself,
i
successfully
spat on
the grave dirt
of
every woman
whose
skin i wore
before
waking up
inside
this one.

- *they didn't deserve this.*

- what i have left for you.

if
my poetry
classes
taught me

anything
about this
life,
it's that

you were the
ted hughes
to my
sylvia plath

& now he's
the robert browning
to my
elizabeth barrett.

- *he dropkicked my heart back to life.*

love does not need to be tragic in order for it to be good. the truth is that i would much rather stir to the feeling of his lips meeting my forehead at 5:30 a.m. every morning for the next eighty odd years than settle for living an eternity alongside someone who can't even be sure where he left his promises the night before.

- fuck those fairy tales.

sometimes
the person
they swear
they'll never
turn into
is the person
who's
always been
standing
before
you.

- *the perfectly woven lie.*

you cannot make the ones with the wanderlust eyes pause in one place—not even if that place has your name etched all over it.

- maps & eXes.

don't
ever doubt
that you
will rise
from
the ruins
of all
the people
who
wanted power
to grow
in their palms
for all
the wrong reasons.

- *this isn't the end yet.*

there's
no such thing
as deserving abuse.

- *let me get "controversial" for a moment.*

who is
more
than
some
kind of
throwaway
backup
plan?

- *you, you, you.*

you
can't settle

for
a single,

always-retreating
wave

when
you deserve

all the
oceans

&
not just

the
cloudy reflection

of them
in the skies.

- *the sun? she told me you are worthy.*

don't
trust
anyone
with a cross hanging
from
their
neck
&
hate
buried
inside
their
chest.

- take it from me.

sometimes
no closure
tells us
more than
the closure
ever
could.

- *some people were never worth your words.*

you're allowed
to give yourself
permission to
fall harder
than the wine
does
into
the bottom
of your glass,
but make sure
you do it
while knowing
there's no one
you should trust
more than
you trust

yourself.

- *gut feelings are a survival tactic.*

there will be
instances

where
you are

the
toxic one—

where
you will need to

step back,
apologize, & reflect.

i know;
i've been the one.

but
even still,

that fact
doesn't

excuse
their abuse.

- *false equivalences.*

i won't let you shut me inside an inescapable yellow room. i won't let you force me to become the keeper of a secret journal hidden underneath a thin mattress. i won't let you tell everyone i'm just a hysterical woman who clung to every word you said & warped them to convince people to join her in a manhunt. this story doesn't end with my silence. this story ends with the yell of every victim who's ever felt hands come behind them to cover their mouth just as the truth started to leak out.

- *come, take back your hatred.*

you
better have
your stakes
in hand
when
the
beautiful
monsters
with
fangs & claws
come
running
towards
you.

- *we're in this together.*

this was the
sun-filled sky.

these were the
singing blackbirds.

these were the
empty pews.

this was the
cracked piano.

this was the
choking choir.

these were the
withered roses.

this was my
little black dress.

these were my
tear-dry cheeks.

this was my
red lipstick grin.

this was your
silent eulogy.

this was your
word-wrapped coffin.

&
this—

this was how
i took myself back.

- *like it or not.*

"you can have my forgiveness,

but you can't have me."

- *the princess saves herself in this one*

acknowledgments

first, i want to thank the enormously talented illustrator of this book, *munise sertel*. this story wouldn't have been complete without your beautiful mark on it. from the very beginning you understood my vision & helped make this book the very best possible version of itself, & for that i will always be grateful.

as always, i want to thank my spouse, *cyrus parker*, who happens to be the sun-heart who appears in the last section of this book. thank you for convincing me to resurrect the chapbook this book was eventually birthed from, even when i didn't think it was possible—ESPECIALLY because i didn't think it was possible. you are what gives me the motivation to do most things in this life. <3

this book wouldn't have seen the light of day without *christine day*. in fact, none of my books would. there isn't a piece of writing that goes out into the world without you seeing it first. i trust you with my life, & more important, my words. i would be lost without your guidance, my writing cheerleader, & my best friend.

my beta readers are incredibly important to the readability of my books. my deepest appreciation to everyone else who helped me push this story in the right direction: *mira kennedy, trista mateer, sophia elaine hanson, & alex andrina.* it was an honor to work with you on this fickle monster of a book.

aaron kent, thank you for writing the poem that inspired my piece titled "our quiet understanding," on page 100. this wasn't the first time you inspired a piece that went into one of my books, & it probably won't be the last! (the first version of this poem originally appeared on aaron's website, poetic interviews. you can visit *poeticinterviews.wordpress.com* to read that poem & more.)

to *my dad, my stepmom, & my sisters* for their outpouring of support when it comes to my writerly endeavors. i couldn't do any of this without knowing you were all on my side. please hear me when i say: thank you. thank you. thank you. thank you. thank you. thank you. thank you. thank you. thank you.

a special thank you to a few people whose enthusiasm for my work keeps me blooming: *danika stone, gretchen gomez, nikita gill, lang leav, caitlyn siehl, iain s. thomas, k.y. robinson, shauna sinyard, summer webb, & olivia paez.* i'm most likely forgetting so many of you, but just know i'm grateful for you, if you're reading this.

thank you to *the bookselling team at the barnes & noble in holmdel, new jersey,* for treating my books as if they were their own children. in fact, a massive thank you to the company in general for treating my book with such love & kindness—both online & off.

to my editor, *patty rice.* to my marketing manager, *holly stayton.* to the rest of *my family at andrews mcmeel publishing.* thank you for loving my work. thank you for trusting me. above all, thank you all so incredibly much for giving me & my books a home where i know we will be kept safe & sound.

& finally . . . thank you, *dear readers,* for taking the time to read my words. for every photo. for every drawing. for every poem. for every comment. for every message. for every email. for every letter. just—thank you. your very existence gives me comfort.

about the author

growing up a word-devourer & avid fairy tale lover, it was only natural that amanda lovelace began writing books of her own, & so she did. when she isn't reading or writing, she can be found waiting for pumpkin spice coffee to come back into season & binge-watching *gilmore girls*. (before you ask: team jess all the way.) the lifelong poetess & storyteller currently lives in new jersey with her spouse, their bunnycat, & a combined book collection so large it will soon need its own home. she has her BA in english literature with a minor in sociology. her first poetry collection, *the princess saves herself in this one*, won the goodreads choice award for best poetry of 2016 & is a *usa today* and *publishers weekly* bestseller.

index

Andrews McMeel Publishing
a division of Andrews McMeel Universal
1130 Walnut Street, Kansas City, Missouri 64106

www.andrewsmcmeel.com

18 19 20 21 22 SDB 10 9 8 7 6 5 4 3 2 1

ISBN: 978-1-4494-9426-1

Library of Congress Control Number: 2018941272

Illustrations by Munise Sertel

Editor: Patty Rice
Designer/Art Director: Julie Barnes
Production Editor: Dave Shaw
Production Manager: Cliff Koehler